3 Minute Prayers

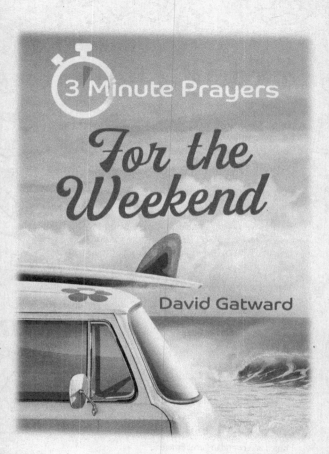

3 Minute Prayers

For the Weekend

David Gatward

kevin
mayhew

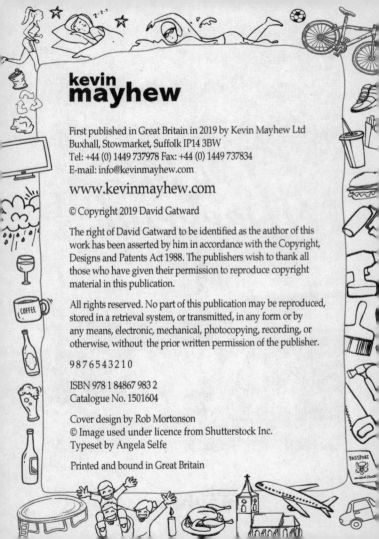

kevin
mayhew

First published in Great Britain in 2019 by Kevin Mayhew Ltd
Buxhall, Stowmarket, Suffolk IP14 3BW
Tel: +44 (0) 1449 737978 Fax: +44 (0) 1449 737834
E-mail: info@kevinmayhew.com

www.kevinmayhew.com

9 8 7 6 5 4 3 2 1 0

ISBN 978 1 84867 983 2
Catalogue No. 1501604

Cover design by Rob Mortonson
© Image used under licence from Shutterstock Inc.
Typeset by Angela Selfe

Printed and bound in Great Britain

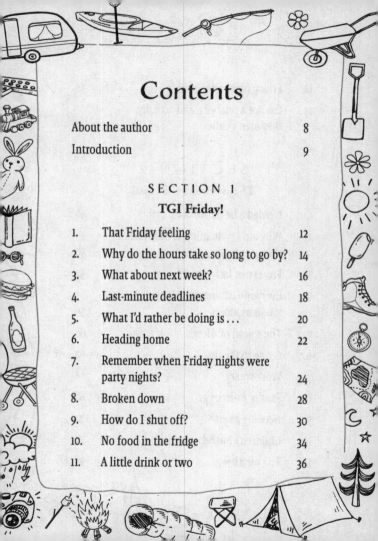

Contents

About the author   8

Introduction   9

SECTION 1
TGI Friday!

1.   That Friday feeling   12
2.   Why do the hours take so long to go by?   14
3.   What about next week?   16
4.   Last-minute deadlines   18
5.   What I'd rather be doing is …   20
6.   Heading home   22
7.   Remember when Friday nights were party nights?   24
8.   Broken down   28
9.   How do I shut off?   30
10.   No food in the fridge   34
11.   A little drink or two   36

| 12. | Friday night television | 38 |
| 13. | I'm not a celebrity, and actually, they aren't either | 42 |

SECTION 2

The weekend – at last!

1.	Needed a lie-in, woke up early	46
2.	Why am I swimming at this time of the morning?	50
3.	Fitness, or lack thereof	52
4.	Everyone's doing triathlons and tough mudders	56
5.	The sound of silence	60
6.	Going to the tip	62
7.	Work-weary	66
8.	Family gatherings	68
9.	Needing a rest	72
10.	Children's birthday parties	74
11.	The weather	78

12.	Holiday traffic	82
13.	Sunday lunch	84
14.	Time to pray	86
15.	I must entertain my children	90
16.	Why don't I like ANY church?	94
17.	Back-to-work blues	98
18.	Trampoline (gasp . . . pant) parks	100

About the author

David had his first book published when he was only 18, before heading off to college to train as an outdoor education specialist. Since then, he's worked on a salmon farm, managed a short-lived magazine, worked in various publishing roles, ghost-written for a best-selling author, written numerous books for children, teenagers and adults, and he is now Managing Director of Kevin Mayhew Publishers.

Introduction

One thing I always find myself tripping up with when it comes to prayer is this idea that everything I say must be utterly profound. It must have depth and meaning and gravitas. It must be about big issues, important issues, world-changing issues. Life and death kind of stuff. Perhaps you're the same? The feeling that every time you pray it must, above all, be all of that and, if possible, more. Because that's the only stuff God listens to, right? This is the Creator we're talking about here, and if we want to be heard then it's not just a case of praying loudest, but praying hardest. And in this, I wonder if there is a confusion. Perhaps it's not so much that prayer must be profound, but that the very nature of it is profound. Trying to make it even more profound is not just impossible, it's pointless.

Prayer is a profound thing. It's God wanting to be in relationship with us, opening up a communication channel and saying, 'Right, tell me about your day. Help me to understand it and be a part of it.' So, take this book as an attempt at doing just that. Because one thing it isn't is profound. And I didn't want it to be. I wanted it to be me asking God into my every day. The little moments. The small experiences. The annoyances that niggle. The kind of things that a weekend involves which is family and tip trips and walks and weariness and work worries and finding time and trying to do too much with the time, and friends and, well, just LIFE!

God wants to be a part of our lives, an absolutely integral part. In the same way that with a close friend you don't just talk to them when you're about to head off for a life-saving operation or if someone's died. No. Instead, that friendship is actually built on the little moments, the small things shared, the everything-about-you. Shouldn't it be so much more with God? Shouldn't we be desperate to ping up a prayer about absolutely everything we're doing? Only you can answer that for yourself. For me, if God wants to be involved in my weekends, then this is the kind of stuff he has to be a part of, and I'm not just ok with that, I think that's pretty much what it's all about.

SECTION 1
TGI Friday!

1

That Friday feeling

It's TGI time, Lord.
The computer screen in front of me
isn't holding my attention.
It should but, you know . . .
I've a few things to do,
and plenty that I'll bump to next week.
All I can think of is getting in the car
and heading home.

The thing I need to make sure of, though,
is that I don't take next week's worries with me.
Life is busy.
It's easy to let it all take over and crowd in
and push everything else out,
like family and friends and relaxing
and walks and reading and laughter
and just thinking and mooching
and hugs and little naps
and garden time
and you.

We need to rest, Lord.
That's one lesson from creation, right?
Do all that work, but take time to step back,
just let everything flow on by for a moment.
Breathe . . .

So that's what I'm going to do.
This weekend, I shall breathe.
And with each breath
I'll remember that even you rested.

Amen

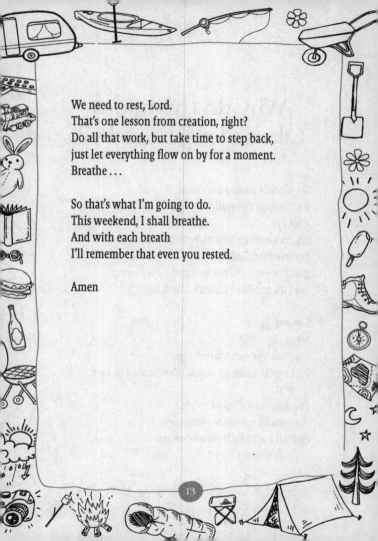

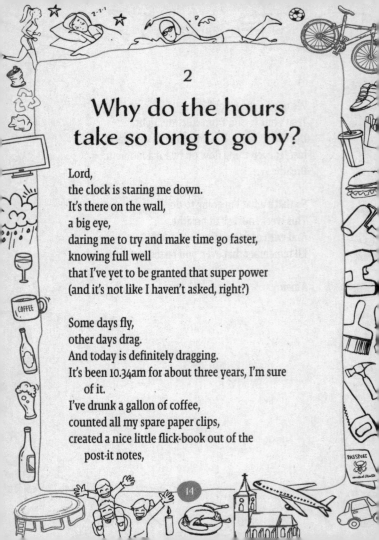

2

Why do the hours take so long to go by?

Lord,
the clock is staring me down.
It's there on the wall,
a big eye,
daring me to try and make time go faster,
knowing full well
that I've yet to be granted that super power
(and it's not like I haven't asked, right?)

Some days fly,
other days drag.
And today is definitely dragging.
It's been 10.34am for about three years, I'm sure
    of it.
I've drunk a gallon of coffee,
counted all my spare paper clips,
created a nice little flick-book out of the
    post-it notes,

and checked all the unread emails in my inbox.
How can it not be lunch?
How can it not be the end of the day?
How can it not be time to go home and crack
    open a beer?

Ooh, look: it's 10.35!
Right, back to work, Lord.
Can't stay chatting to you all day, can I?
(I'll call again in five, ok?)

Amen

3

What about next week?

Next week is terrifying, Lord.
This week was busy,
but next?
The only way I can survive it
is to not sleep.
Not that I sleep that well as it is,
but there you go.

There's meetings to go to,
things to plan and sort and execute,
new stuff to deal with,
old stuff to face.
My head hurts just thinking about it,
probably because I'm banging it against a wall . . .

I worry too much, Lord.
Always have.
I keep it well hidden most times,

but when that worry bubbles up,
sometimes it comes out as something else entirely:
frustration;
annoyance;
anger.

None of those are good.
They're like the secret ugly siblings of worry,
just waiting for an excuse
to say 'hi'.

Right, I need to prioritise.
Sitting here worrying won't solve anything.
Lists!
I need lists, Lord!
A plan!

It's not next week yet, Lord,
I know,
but help me face it now.

Amen

4

Last-minute deadlines

Deadlines, last-minute deadlines.
How I just love them. Not!
And so-called urgent, can't-possibly-wait
    till-Monday-morning requests.
It's the middle of the afternoon
and a demand has just come in, Lord,
for some 'figures'...
Because, as we all know,
everyone wants to look at figures late on a Friday,
then take them home to look at over the weekend,
right?

No.

Not me, anyway.
But here I am, trying to get this together,
stay focused,
and ignore the clock ticking the seconds away.

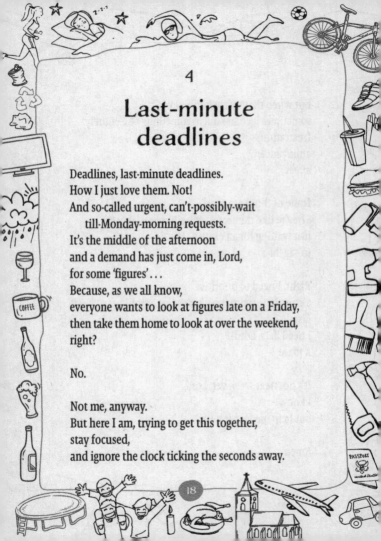

Not easy,
not when I've got such a great weekend ahead!
It's a busy one, Lord.
Friends, an evening out, bit of a day trip.
Can't wait!
And neither can these figures,
or more importantly,
the person who asked for them.

Right, best knuckle down.
See you at the end of this spreadsheet, Lord.

Amen

5

What I'd rather be doing is...

Lord,
I'm lucky enough to have green fields outside my
    office window.
When I get a moment's break
I stare off into the middle distance
and think about anything that just pops into
    my head.
Sometimes it's a book I'm reading,
other times it's a person or a place.
But now?
Right now, it's crowded in there,
because there are a million things I'd rather be doing
than this!

I'm lucky, Lord,
and I know that.
I have a job to pay the bills
and a little bit left over to enjoy.
So I'm not being ungrateful.

But it doesn't mean that every moment of every day
is filled with joy.
It isn't.
And right now
there are so many other things I'd rather be doing!

I don't need to list them, Lord.
You know them as well as I do.
And actually,
if you think about it,
the fact that I've got that list,
that I have so many other things that I can and
    will be doing.
Well, that's pretty amazing, isn't it?

Perhaps, then,
right now,
even though there are plenty of other things I'd
    rather be doing,
I should focus on what I have to be doing instead,
because if I wasn't doing this right now,
then I probably wouldn't be able to do a lot of them
when it finishes.

Amen

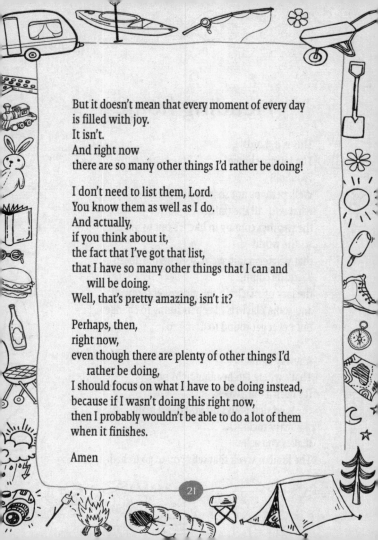

6

Heading home

This is it, Lord!
The journey home!
Woohoo!
Well, perhaps not so 'woohoo',
what with all the traffic,
the weather coming in like it's out to prove to
    the world
that whatever rain we've seen before doesn't
    really count,
the lack of snacks in the passenger footwell,
and some playlists I keep meaning to change
but never get round to doing so.

Anyway, home . . .
That's where I'm heading right now.
It's been a long week,
the kind that hangs off you like a really
    heavy rucksack,
makes you ache.
The kind of week that tells you to go to bed,

that you need to sleep,
but doesn't let you.

So I'm yawning, Lord,
and ahead of me the road stretches to home.
Between here and there I'll pass thousands
     of others,
doing the same,
all heading home,
all tired.
Some will have had good weeks,
others not so much.
Some will be looking forward to getting home,
others dreading it
(and I've experienced that a fair few times, as you
     well know.)

Help us all to drive safely, Lord,
and arrive.

Amen

7

Remember when Friday nights were party nights?

Yeah! Friday night, Lord!
PARTAY!
Or not.
Frankly, now I'm home,
the only kind of party I want
is one that involves getting my feet up
and falling asleep to a movie
with a glass of wine in my hand.
I'm wild now, right?

Sometimes,
I find myself looking back to those 'see it through
    till dawn' days,
and wish that I could still do it.
I start to believe that those were the best times ever,
that because I don't have them any more
I'm boring and dull and really not very exciting at all.

But then I'm also no longer 21.
No bad thing.

I guess I do this as much as anyone:
look back on old times
and decide they were the good times,
almost as though the times I'm experiencing now
just don't match up.
And that's nonsense.

Right now, Lord?
Well, life's good.
Yeah, it's got its bad stuff,
its dull stuff,
stuff that makes my head hurt,
but all in all,
I'm lucky, Lord.

Life's not less exciting than it was,
it's different, in an exciting way!
So I don't head out on Friday nights
to see if I can see it through till dawn,
but so much has taken its place.

And I need to accept that change is a good thing,
to embrace it,
because without it,
how can I ever really become
the 'me' you know I can be?

Amen

3 Minute Prayers

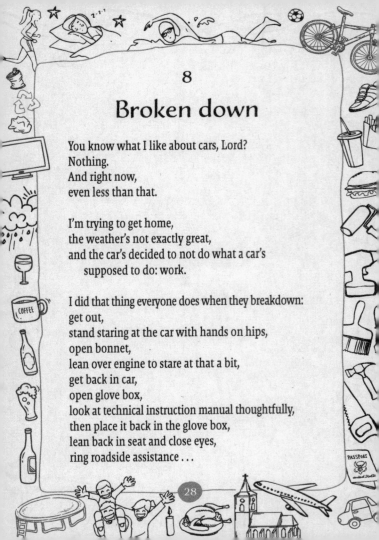

8

Broken down

You know what I like about cars, Lord?
Nothing.
And right now,
even less than that.

I'm trying to get home,
the weather's not exactly great,
and the car's decided to not do what a car's
    supposed to do: work.

I did that thing everyone does when they breakdown:
get out,
stand staring at the car with hands on hips,
open bonnet,
lean over engine to stare at that a bit,
get back in car,
open glove box,
look at technical instruction manual thoughtfully,
then place it back in the glove box,
lean back in seat and close eyes,
ring roadside assistance . . .

So, I've two hours to kill,
on a Friday night,
at the side of the road.

I'm too dependent on this mechanical marvel, Lord.
Gets on my nerves.
But I have to get to work,
and public transport doesn't work for the journey
    I do.
So it's either this
or a horse.
And I don't think my garden's big enough for
    a horse,
not even one of those tiny cute ones.

First world problem, I know.
I'm complaining that the decent car I have,
which takes me to a job I have,
isn't working.
It's hardly the end of the world.

Time to get things into perspective I think, right?
And perhaps have a little roadside nap ...

Amen

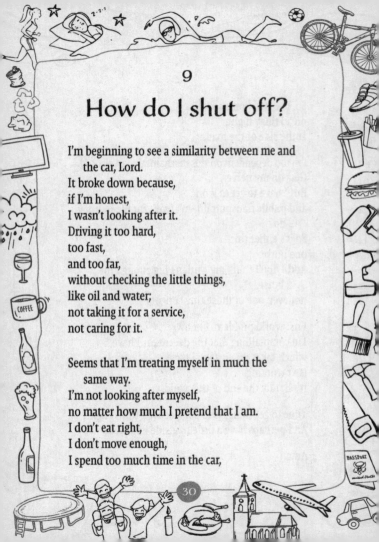

9

How do I shut off?

I'm beginning to see a similarity between me and
  the car, Lord.
It broke down because,
if I'm honest,
I wasn't looking after it.
Driving it too hard,
too fast,
and too far,
without checking the little things,
like oil and water;
not taking it for a service,
not caring for it.

Seems that I'm treating myself in much the
  same way.
I'm not looking after myself,
no matter how much I pretend that I am.
I don't eat right,
I don't move enough,
I spend too much time in the car,

I don't exercise properly.
But then, who does?
I'm no gym freak.
I don't have the time.
My life has no routine.
So trying to do anything sensible just doesn't
    seem to work.
And anyway, I'm way too busy,
and I'll just have to try later in the year,
when things calm down . . .

. . . by which point
I'll be a broken mess.

I've got one body, Lord.
I need to look after it,
feed it,
exercise it,
help it work as well as it should.
To stop making excuses,
and to start making changes.

Right, where are those running shoes, Lord?
I've found this app on my phone,
'Couch to 5k'...
Worth a try, right?

Amen

3 Minute Prayers

10

No food in the fridge

Got those late-night munchies, Lord,
but the fridge is empty.
Well, it's not empty as such,
I mean there are vegetables in there,
and a pot or two of something suspicious,
milk,
a bit of cheese . . .
So, not exactly empty,
but hardly the veritable feast
that my it's-nearly-midnight hunger pangs
    are demanding.

I've an urge to create a massive sandwich.
And it must contain many ingredients!
I'm not talking a little bit of Dairylea cheese here.
No.
I'm talking peanut butter and crisps and cheese and
    ham and pickle and . . .
Basically, the kind of sandwich that could put your
    jaw out of whack.

Doesn't look like I'm going to be able to create
   that right now, does it?
But my weekend demands it!
I've managed to stay up later than expected,
there's a movie on,
it's a commercial break,
and I've got the munchies!

A part of me thinks it's pointless telling you stuff
   like this,
but then, isn't this what friends do?
Just chat?
I don't suddenly stop talking to a friend
when what we're talking about isn't
      life-changing, right?
So why should it be any different with you?

It shouldn't.
It isn't.

Back to the sandwich,
or lack of one.
Looks like it's just a bag of crisps for me, then, Lord.

Amen

11

A little drink or two

Lord,
I like a drink.
There, I've admitted it.
I do.
And at the weekend,
it's rather nice to open a bottle of red,
or have a few beers,
or a snifter of whisky.

Problem is,
and I've noticed this for sure these past
    few months,
that a few nice drinks at the weekend have,
with very little effort,
become a few nice drinks through the week.

Looking back at the last few days,
I've drunk every night.
Not loads.
I'm not getting slammed.

But I am drinking.
A few beers here,
half a bottle of wine there,
a whisky to send me off to bed.

That's not good, is it?
It's an easy thing to fall into, though, Lord.
A habit that's comforting,
something to look forward to at the end of the day.
But I need to get this under control.
It's not that it's out of control now,
but I can see how it soon could be.
And if you think about the health implications,
the cost of it . . .
Not big, or clever.

So, perhaps,
I'll put this beer back in the fridge,
and just head to bed . . .

Amen

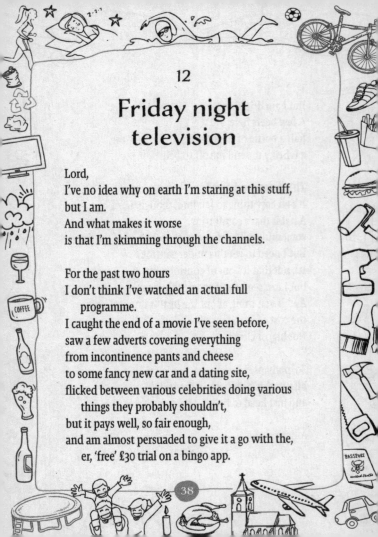

12

Friday night television

Lord,
I've no idea why on earth I'm staring at this stuff,
but I am.
And what makes it worse
is that I'm skimming through the channels.

For the past two hours
I don't think I've watched an actual full
　　programme.
I caught the end of a movie I've seen before,
saw a few adverts covering everything
from incontinence pants and cheese
to some fancy new car and a dating site,
flicked between various celebrities doing various
　　things they probably shouldn't,
but it pays well, so fair enough,
and am almost persuaded to give it a go with the,
　　er, 'free' £30 trial on a bingo app.

I've spent my time better than this, that's for sure.
Can't say I'm that proud, really.
All time is precious,
and these two hours are ones that I've done
nothing with at all.
Yes, I'm tired,
yes, I fancy just slobbing about for a bit,
but is this really the best I can do?

What makes it worse is that I've done it before
and I'll do it again.
The television will draw me in,
the adverts will hypnotise me,
the numerous channels beckon me onwards to
keep surfing
till I find something worth watching.

I need to get a control on this, right?
It's not a good use of my time.
Relaxing doesn't have to be massively productive,
but neither should it be just a total waste.
I mean, here's an idea:
what if I just read a book?

Seriously! An actual book!
How much better would that be than this
    right now?
(Don't answer that.)

Right,
a book . . .
I've a bookshelf rammed with the things after all,
loads I've not read.
Time to switch off that television
and do something less boring instead . . .

Amen

3 Minute Prayers

I'm not a celebrity, and actually, they aren't either

Here's a weird thing, Lord:
apparently, being a 'celebrity' is now a
    career choice.
Like it's an actual thing
rather than something attached to something
    you've done,
or are good at, are known for.
I've even heard that children are saying
it's what they want to be when they grow up.
Not doctors or tree surgeons or care workers
or soldiers or teachers or accountants or nurses
or – add basically every other job in the world
    which is an actual job, Lord,
but 'celebrities'.

How is this even a thing?
'I want to be a celebrity.'

What *is* that?
I mean, all it is, right, is that lots of people know
    who you are.
Oh, and somehow, you end up getting paid for it.

Strikes me as a bit weird.
And a bit wrong.
What use is a person famous for being famous?
They're used for advertising,
but that's hardly world-changing.

Look, I'm not saying that everyone must have
    a calling,
that every person must have a fulfilling job,
that every job must serve a real and true purpose
    in society,
but 'celebrity' . . .
can't get my head around it.
Not sure I want to, either,
probably because I can't imagine anything worse,
the idea of everyone knowing who you are,
what you're about,
what you're up to.

But then this is the world of reality TV,
of everyone being interconnected,
where we all share our lives, usually intimately,
online.

This is one of those prayers, Lord,
where there's no real conclusion,
no real reason to pray it.
It's just something I'm trying to work through,
    I guess.
I live in a society that celebrates the simple notion
    of celebrity,
puts it above almost everything else,
and if I'm going to have any chance of living in
    that society,
and understanding it,
then I need to work out my own views about it.
Help me do that, Lord.

Amen

SECTION 2

The weekend
- at last!

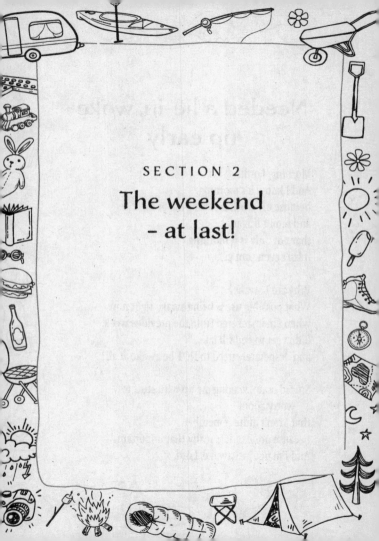

1

Needed a lie-in, woke up early

Morning, Lord!
And I know it's morning,
because my clock is staring me in the face
and reminding me
that not only is it morning,
it isn't even 5am yet.

Why am I awake?
What possible use is being awake right now,
when I'm knackered from the previous week,
didn't get to bed till late,
and desperately need to NOT be awake at all?

Stupid brain, waking me up with stuff to
        worry about
that I can't quite remember
because none of it is really that important.
And I'm not just awake, Lord,

but wide awake,
like I won't ever need to sleep again!

Now I'm getting restless.
But if I get up,
I'll wake the rest of the house up,
and that's never good.
But I can't just lie here,
staring at the ceiling,
or I'll go nuts!

Right,
I'm going to give it a go.
I'm going to get up,
sneak downstairs,
and do something useful.
I'm not quite sure what that is yet,
but I'll think of something.
Might even go for a walk . . .

Actually,
that's exactly what I'm going to do.

It's looking foggy out there,
dawn is on its way so it's still darkish . . .
Yeah, a walk would be good.
Go have a look at the world at a time when I'm
    usually asleep.
I'll leave a note on the table,
go for a stroll,
come back in time for breakfast.

Ha! I'm actually rather excited now!
How funny is that?
Just the simple act of going for an early
    morning walk,
breaking my routine,
doing something different,
and I somehow, for some reason, feel better
about whatever is was that was worrying me
enough to wake me up early.

Right, out we go, Lord . . .

Amen

3 Minute Prayers

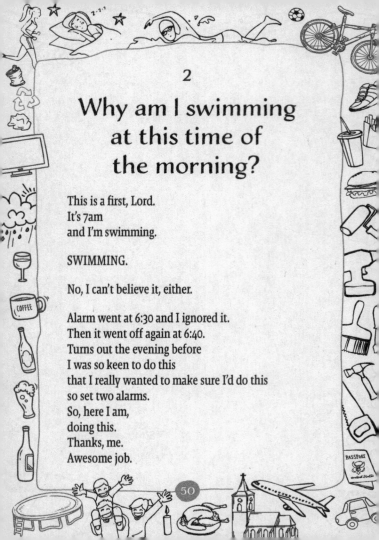

2

Why am I swimming at this time of the morning?

This is a first, Lord.
It's 7am
and I'm swimming.

SWIMMING.

No, I can't believe it, either.

Alarm went at 6:30 and I ignored it.
Then it went off again at 6:40.
Turns out the evening before
I was so keen to do this
that I really wanted to make sure I'd do this
so set two alarms.
So, here I am,
doing this.
Thanks, me.
Awesome job.

At least the pool's pretty empty.
No surprise really;
only people as stupid as me
would do this.

The thing is,
that even though I'm complaining,
and even though it's early and I'm tired
and I can't believe I'm here
when most folk are sensibly still in bed,
I can't help but feel rather good about myself.
I'll be out of here and back home just after 8,
and I'll have already done something awesome
before most folk are even out of bed and in
    the shower!
Maybe I should do this again next week!
Maybe I should do this every day!

Hmmm . . . best to not get carried away.
Anyway, I'm not even in the pool yet.

Right, here goes:
an early-morning swim . . .

Amen

3

Fitness, or lack thereof

See this, Lord?
This card in my hand?
It's a gym membership!
Yes!
I've done it!
I've joined a gym!
And in three months' time
I'll be as fit as a fit thing!
Well, that's what the photographs around the
    gym would have me believe.
Not sure it is.
Not sure I want to go at all.
Maybe I won't . . .

But that's why I paid for a membership, right?
To give me that push to get myself into shape.
Otherwise, it's just a waste of money.
At least that's what I'm telling myself.

I've had my induction,
been given a programme to follow,
shown how to use the equipment.
I'll be honest,
it's terrifying.
And you want to know the reason why?
Because I'm embarrassed.
I don't want to go because I'm unfit
and a bit wobbly
and absolutely everyone else at the gym
is the opposite.
Well, they're not,
but you know what I mean.

I don't want to get changed,
because someone will see what I look like.
I don't want to go into the gym,
because someone will see just how unfit I am.
Perhaps I'm better just to turn around,
head home, never come back ...

Silly really, Lord,
to care so much about what other people think.

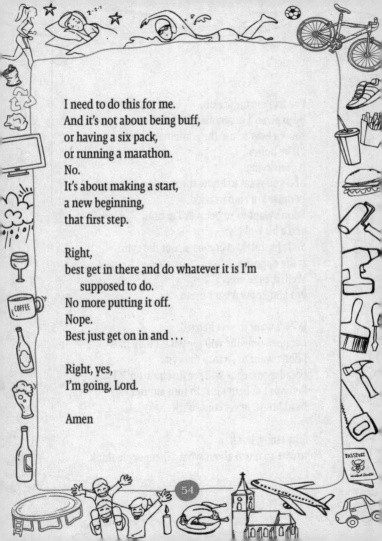

I need to do this for me.
And it's not about being buff,
or having a six pack,
or running a marathon.
No.
It's about making a start,
a new beginning,
that first step.

Right,
best get in there and do whatever it is I'm
    supposed to do.
No more putting it off.
Nope.
Best just get on in and . . .

Right, yes,
I'm going, Lord.

Amen

4

Everyone's doing triathlons and tough mudders

Lord,
I can't keep up.
I've tried,
I really have,
but whatever I do,
there's always someone faster or stronger or fitter,
someone who can swim or run or cycle faster,
lift more weight.
It's getting on my nerves.
And it seems that wherever I turn
the people around me are doing something
  more impressive:
someone's doing a marathon;
someone else is doing a triathlon;
a friend of a friend is doing an 'ultra' (whatever
  that is, right?).

I'm just me, Lord.
I need to get fit,
to lose a bit of weight,
yet all these folk around me make me start to
   think that it's not enough.
I need to be like them,
to push myself further and harder and harder
   and further.
But I'm not an athlete, Lord!
I never won a race at school,
I'm never going to break any records,
and there's no way on earth
I'm ever going to be faster or stronger
or whatever than any of these people, and that's
   a fact!

I feel a little disappointed, to be honest.
I'd like to be like them.
I really would.
It must be amazing to be that good at something.
Me?

I'm just a plodder.
I'm just trying to do the best that I can,
with the time that I have.

Is that good enough, Lord?
Actually, what *is* good enough?
Do you want me to be like them,
to aim for excellence?
Or is what I'm doing excellence enough?
Does excellence even count?
And is exercise really exercise
unless you use the words 'extreme' or 'ultra' in
    front of it?

I'm not perfect, Lord.
I'm just someone trying to move a little more than
    they used to,
to look after myself a little better,
to eat healthier,
to exercise.

And I hope that's enough.
Because if the only way to get into heaven is to
    complete a triathlon,
then I'm throwing the towel in right now . . .

Amen

5

The sound of silence

Lord,
I'm taking a moment.
It's a beautiful day,
I'm outside,
and the world is peaceful.

It's the weekend and I'm trying to get my head
together again.
A bit of peace and quiet doesn't half do wonders
for the soul.
Silence...
Except that the sound of silence is so rich, isn't it?
I mean,
if I listen really carefully,
I can hear birds and distant cars and a plane
and some voices and wind in the trees
and the sound of my own breathing...

What I'm trying to do
is let those sounds slip into my head for a while

and push out all the other stuff that fills it up with
   too much noise.
That noise can be anything,
the general noise of life,
of things I need to do,
people I need to see,
decisions I have to make,
stuff that needs to be done.
It's busy in my head, Lord.
Noisy.

Time for a deep breath . . .
To feel it
and to hear it.
Time to take a moment . . .
to let things just flow on by for a while,
to drift a little in the silence around me.

Amen

6

Going to the tip

Lord,
there is no more thankless task
than heading off on a warm, sunny
    Saturday morning,
with a car full of rubbish,
to sit in a queue
to the tip.
But that's what I'm doing right now, Lord.
I've made better decisions about my mornings,
    I must say.

I don't even know where any of the stuff I'm
    throwing out came from.
And what makes it even worse is that I've just
    moved house
and I swore I would absolutely not move a load
    of rubbish from one place
to another,
just so that I would then have to go and
    do exactly

what I'm doing now
a few weeks later.

I'm a product of my own stupidity, I guess.
And the back of the car is stuffed with products
    of the product of my own stupidity,
if you get what I mean.
I was looking through it all and wondering why
    I had it,
what use it had ever been,
why I'd not got rid of it years ago.
I know for a fact that there are more mornings
    like this ahead of me.
More rubbish to sort or to discover and to
    throw out.

It's such a waste, Lord.
I fill my life with 'stuff' and the 'stuff' piles up
and I put it in boxes and the boxes get put
    on shelves
and when the shelves are full they get put in the
    loft or the shed or the garage

and then they get lost behind other boxes
and soon, before you know it, there I am, living
    in a post-apocalyptic future
where everything is in boxes and . . .
Sorry, got carried away,
but you get what I mean, right?

All this stuff, Lord,
and none of it of use to me or to anyone.
Oh, look,
the gate's open,
and we're moving at last.

I wonder if there's some internal rubbish I need
    to deal with, Lord?
Sort through a few things,
find that stuff I'm hanging on to that I shouldn't.
I'm not going to get all heavy here,
but there are things tucked way down deep
that I shouldn't be carrying around any more.
Perhaps, with these boxes that I'm ditching,
I should ditch a few things from the inside, too.

Just a few to begin with,
nothing too shocking.
Start small, right?

Time to clear away the rubbish, Lord.

Amen

7

Work-weary

I shouldn't be thinking about next week,
but I am.
I'm supposed to be relaxing,
but I'm not.

On the outside, I'm doing a very good
    impression of
'Yeah, everything's fine, just great!'
But on the inside?
Right now, I feel like I'm drowning.

I need to sort this out, Lord.
I need to take time out.
I need to relax,
I need to take stock,
I need to breathe in some peace.

Last week was last week.
Worrying about next week won't change anything.
Actually, it will:

it'll change what's supposed to be a good weekend
into one that isn't.
And that's a change I don't want.
And it's absolutely one I don't need.

Right,
deep breath,
put all that stuff to one side, right?
And, if you don't mind me asking, Lord,
can I place it all in your hands?
I'm not asking you to solve it,
I'm not asking for miracles,
I'm just asking that you look over it,
so that when I come to face it,
I'll know that you're there with me as well?

Thanks.

Amen

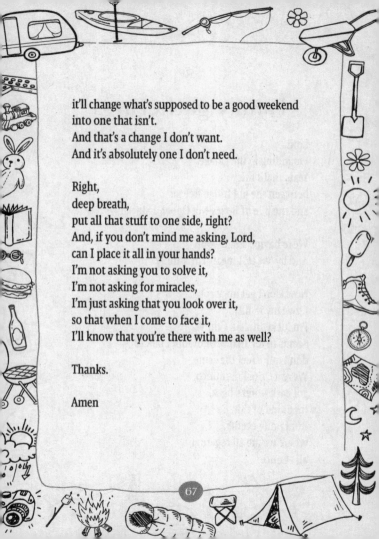

8

Family gatherings

Lord,
I'm hiding in the garage.
Yeah, that's me:
between the old fridge-freezer
and the pile of Boxes Not Opened Since 1998 . . .

We're having a barbeque.
And by 'we're' I mean The Family.

Now, don't get me wrong,
I love my family.
I'm lucky in that, I think.
Seems to me that a lot of folk I talk to
don't quite feel the same.
We're a close-knit bunch,
got each other's back,
that kind of thing.
But family events,
where we are all together
all at once

all at the same time . . .
It can't half be a bit stressful, Lord.

You see,
we may love each other,
but bring those now separate lives
    crashing together?
It's a recipe not so much for disaster
but for a lot of pressure on the event to be at
    least amazing
and if not that, then fantastic will do.

The differences show up pretty quickly,
the differences of opinion,
the ways of doing things,
the little habits and whatnot that you know
    shouldn't annoy,
but still do.
Then there's the photos,
the food everyone brings (or doesn't),
the who's-doing-which-bit organising,
the what-to-do-with-the-kids,

the guess-who's-late-again . . .
It's exhausting.

Which is why I'm out here, hiding in the garage.
I need a breather, Lord.
Just a moment or two to get my head together.
Get my game-face on.
Family is important, Lord.
And I'm blessed with something many don't have.
Help me not to ruin it
by seeing the imperfections as a problem
rather than a necessary part
of what it is to be us.

You love us as we are, right?
We should do the same.

Amen

9

Needing a rest

Lord,
I've spent the whole week looking forward to
 this weekend,
because, rather foolishly,
I thought I'd be able to use it to relax a little.
How wrong could I be?

Here's the mix:
Broken-down washing machine.
Tip run.
Shopping.
School sports event.
Visit by friends (who aren't really, but for
 whatever reason we or they insist on keeping
 in touch).
Visit to family.
And some other stuff I've forgotten or blanked
 from my memory already,
even though we've not done it all yet.

Is this a first-world problem?
Yeah, I guess so.
How lucky am I to have a weekend to even think
    as potentially being a chance to rest and relax?
Hugely.
I need to remember that.

Right,
tip run done,
shopping done,
time to throw a toasted sandwich into my face
before the rest of the day attacks.

Amen

10

Children's birthday parties

Lord,
hate is a strong word.
I know that.
I know that I shouldn't 'hate'.
But this?
This I really do: children's birthday parties.

When did it become a competition?
Who decided that we must all try to outdo other
    families with the grandeur of The Party?
No longer is 'having some friends around' enough.
Parties have gone way beyond some
    rubbish games,
a few cheap presents, and a massive cake.
Now we've got all kinds of crazy.
I've taken my two to everything from paint-balling
to a falconry experience to go-karting.

These are things I expect on the list for a
    stag weekend,
not for a bunch of tweens celebrating a birthday.

Also,
and I admit this freely and openly,
I'm not a massive fan of the whole 'let's all be
    friends' approach to meeting the parents of the
    other children.
There's only so much polite conversation I can
    deal with.
And more often than not
the conversation is either about our children (yawn)
or work/business (yawn).

And the worst thing of all?
The absolute crux of the why-I-don't-like-
    children's-birthday-parties thing?
That it's no longer something that happens after
    school for an hour or two.
No.
That's not allowed.

For indeed, a children's birthday party must take
    up at least half, if not a whole day
at the weekend.

No.
No it shouldn't.
Because for me that's family time.
Our time together.
And sometimes it feels like these parties are
    time thieves.

I'm being overly dramatic, I know that.
But sometimes I just need to get these things off
    my chest.
It doesn't necessarily make me feel any better,
but at least someone else knows what's going on
    in my head.
Right,
best get the kids in the car and drive half an hour
to something that undoubtedly cost too much
and probably involves skiing and horse riding

and a visit from a celebrity and a posh meal done
    by a visiting chef.
Or something.

Lord,
give me strength . . .

Amen

11

The weather

Lord,
it's raining.
No surprise there, right?
Well, regardless of that,
I could do with a little bit of sunshine.
Actually, not even that,
just a weekend that doesn't feel like I'm
        spending it
under a soaking wet bath towel.

Look at it out there, Lord.
Horrible.
A grey day,
sheets of rain,
and a chill wind.
Right now,
it's pretty much how I feel inside.
No reason really,
just one of those 'not doing that great' days.

Can't put my finger on it.
Which is why I need a little bit of sun in my life.
That massive ball of fire is quite amazing, really.
Yeah, it does all that stuff that helps plants grow,
and some other sciencey stuff,
but it's amazing what it can do to your state
    of mind.

A break in the clouds,
a single ray of gold shining through the grey,
a day drenched in light and heat . . .
Your mind reacts to it, Lord.
It relaxes,
calms a little,
takes a moment to just 'be'.

Looks like the rain's breaking, Lord.
Well, that's something, right?
Can't rain all the time.
And to be honest,
if it was sunny all the time
that wouldn't work either, would it?

Perhaps, Lord,
these grey days
help me appreciate the bright sunny ones all the
     more.
And the same works the other way around:
too much sun and the world is soon crying out for
     rain.

My life is a mix of bright days and dark days.
Days of rain
and days of sun.
It's what being a human is about.
Well, part of it.
Ups and downs,
good days and bad.
With one constant: you.

Amen

3 Minute Prayers

12

Holiday traffic

Lord,
I've been sitting here for over an hour.
There's no report of an accident.
It's just heavy traffic.
Hundreds and thousands of people as stupid as me
all trying to get to the same place at the same time.

Nonsense.

I planned the journey,
left early,
made sure we had the car packed the night before.
Guess how much difference it's made?
Yep, none.
Not a jot.

It's all I can do not to scream.
Best turn the music up in case I do ...

My biggest problem with traffic, Lord,
is that I always feel like I'm wasting my life.
Spending hours of it crawling along in my car
is not what I should be doing.

Those precious hours,
gone.
Floating off on a haze of car fumes
and odd smells from fast-food vans.

Modern life is a bit odd really.
Spend all that time working
and then when we do have free time
we waste it doing something like this.
And for what?
A few hours at the beach
(which is already hideously overcrowded and the
    exact opposite of relaxing).

Sorry for the winge, Lord.
It'll be worth it in the end, I'm sure.
(Just so long as the car park isn't full,
we haven't forgotten anything,
no one is car sick,
no one steps in dog poop,
I don't get unnecessarily angry about the lengths
    of queues
for food/toilet/car park ticket machine . . .)

Amen

13

Sunday lunch

Lord,
as we gather here, together,
I want us all to realise just how fortunate we are,
and to thank you for it.

We have each other,
we have a home.
We have friends and family.
We are healthy and happy (well, most of
    the time).

I also want us to pause
and to think about all the times we forget all of
    this in front of us.
The moments we compare ourselves to others,
where we envy,
where anger clouds a moment.

This time, Lord,
is not just about food.

It is about us,
together,
and being thankful for just that.

Amen

14

Time to pray

Lord,
finding time to pray
is like finding time to read.
I keep thinking about it,
know how good it is for me,
know that I enjoy it,
even sit down to do it,
then life gets in the way,
and that's the end of that.

Not good.

What I don't want to do
is to have it become some kind of
    timetabled thing.
I'm rubbish with timetables.
Well, I'm very good at making them,
can spend hours/days/weeks doing that bit,
but then when it comes to putting it into action?
Er, no.

Half the problem
is that even now, after so many years,
I'm not sure how to do it,
how often,
if there should be a format,
if I'm doing it wrong . . .
For example,
does this count?
This little prayer now?
Is it enough?
Would it pass the How to Pray test?

I'm not sure you're bothered, really, Lord.
No.
You're more interested in the fact that I pray at all.
And that's what I need to focus on.

I read somewhere a motivational line
    about running.
Goes along the lines of, 'doesn't matter how slow
    you're going, or how far,
it's still faster and further than everyone on
    the couch.'

Perhaps the same applies to prayer?
That I'm doing it at all is something.
It may be sporadic,
it may be rambling and disorganised,
but it's more than not doing it at all.
And that has to count for something.
Hope so, Lord.

Amen

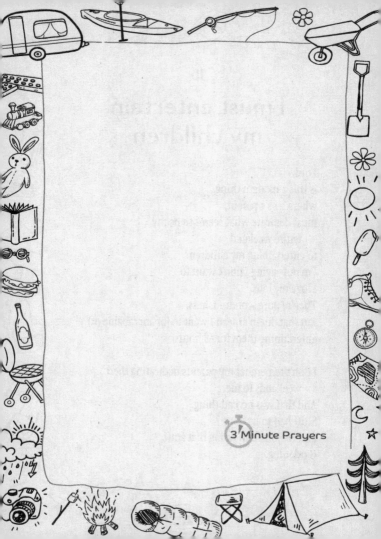

3 Minute Prayers

15

I must entertain my children

Lord,
is this a modern thing,
where I, as a parent,
must dedicate what seems to be my
    entire weekend
to entertaining my children?
I'm not saying I don't want to.
I love my kids.
They're pure wondrousness.
But that doesn't mean I want to (or am capable of)
entertaining them for 48 hours.

I don't remember my parents dedicating their
    weekends to me.
And that was no bad thing.
Stuff had to be done
and we joined in doing that stuff.
Gardening,

fetching firewood,
cooking . . .
(It wasn't all like that, Lord,
I didn't grow up in a Victorian-themed household.)

Now though,
we parents seem to be almost paranoid about
    'doing stuff with the kids'.
And before you know it
this 'doing stuff' involves 'spending money'.
I'm happy to be convinced otherwise,
but I'm sure my offspring will be fine
without visiting every single museum/theme park/
    beach/restaurant/science fair in the land.

So here's what I'm going to do:
I'm going to bring back the simple stuff.
Garage needs clearing?
Let's do that together, then cook lunch.
Garden?
Yep, let's all crack on with it, right?
Then we could go for a walk,
take a flask of hot chocolate . . .

Special family time doesn't mean it has to be an
    epic adventure, Lord.
To be honest,
the most special times are often the simplest,
just time spent together,
regardless of what we're doing.

And that's what it's about, isn't it?
We've replaced time together
with time doing stuff,
and the more amazing,
the more expensive,
the better.

Except that it isn't.
Time together is what it's about,
whatever we're doing.
Because whatever we're doing,
if we're doing it together,
then that's something special right there.

Amen

3 Minute Prayers

16

Why don't I like ANY church?

It's Sunday morning, Lord,
and I don't want to go to church.
I don't enjoy it.
I don't get much out of it.
I don't fit in with the people who attend.
It feels like a chore.

I've tried other churches
and seem to always feel the same,
like I'm a weird piece of a jigsaw puzzle
that can't find the right puzzle that it fits in.

I sound like a moody teenager:
this church is too happy.
That church is too serious.
This church is too modern.
That church is too traditional.

I'm the very definition of difficult to please.

Perhaps the problem is me.
It probably is.
The church isn't just there for me, is it?
And I'm not happy that I'm approaching this as
     a consumer.
I'm starting to believe the hype, it seems:
that my needs are paramount,
the customer is always right,
and I'm the customer here,
and I want comfy seats and coffee
and to not have to give the sign of the peace
or to feel like I must clap in every song or hymn
or to always take communion and . . .

Me, me, me, me, me . . .
How horrendously selfish.
Need to change my attitude.
Nowhere is ever going to be perfect, is it?
Which is why it works.
The church is more human that way.

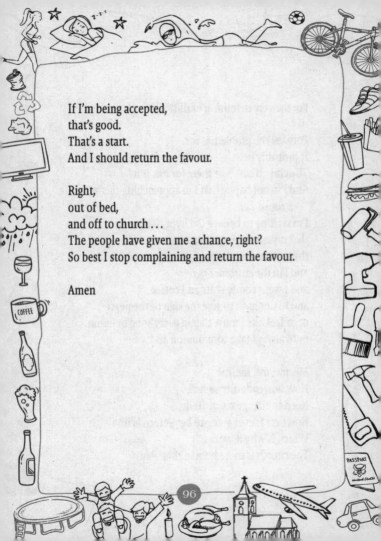

If I'm being accepted,
that's good.
That's a start.
And I should return the favour.

Right,
out of bed,
and off to church ...
The people have given me a chance, right?
So best I stop complaining and return the favour.

Amen

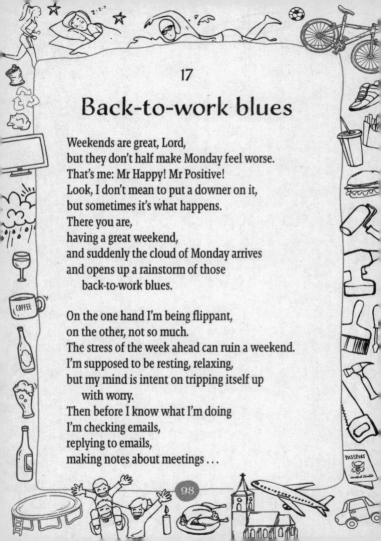

17

Back-to-work blues

Weekends are great, Lord,
but they don't half make Monday feel worse.
That's me: Mr Happy! Mr Positive!
Look, I don't mean to put a downer on it,
but sometimes it's what happens.
There you are,
having a great weekend,
and suddenly the cloud of Monday arrives
and opens up a rainstorm of those
    back-to-work blues.

On the one hand I'm being flippant,
on the other, not so much.
The stress of the week ahead can ruin a weekend.
I'm supposed to be resting, relaxing,
but my mind is intent on tripping itself up
    with worry.
Then before I know what I'm doing
I'm checking emails,
replying to emails,
making notes about meetings . . .

See?
That doesn't make for a relaxing time, does it?
I need to breathe, Lord.
To understand that worrying won't change anything.
Actually it will:
it'll change the weekend from good
to bad.
I'll end up back at work on Monday worse than
    when I left it on Friday.

Time to breathe, Lord.
That's what the weekend is about.
To breathe life in and the stress out.
I just need to learn to leave work at work, Lord,
because that's where it belongs.
Not here, with me now,
surrounded by friends and family.

Help me make the most of these moments, Lord,
because without them
I won't be in any fit state to deal with the week ahead.

Amen

18

Trampoline
(gasp … pant) parks

Lord,
I'm just taking a … breather …
Because if I don't,
I think I might just die.

We're at a trampoline park.
Imagine, if you will, a popcorn machine
the size of a warehouse
filled with children.
That.

Trampolining is fun, apparently.
And I'm sure it is
when you're under the age of 16,
weigh nothing,
and have the energy of a mad puppy on caffeine.

We've been here for 15 minutes.
15!

Another 45 to go.
I've yet to try the slackline,
the sponge pit,
the bit where you bounce on trampolines as
    strangers throw balls at you.
It's . . . exhausting.

I feel like I'm being ambushed by a gang
    armed with weapons that fire small children.
Wherever I turn there are 4-year-olds
    doing tumbles,
tweens racing from trampoline to trampoline,
teenagers doing backflips.
Yes: backflips!
I'm so not doing that.

This is one of those experiences designed only to
    make you feel your age.
And boy, do I feel that right now.
I'm out of breath,
sweating,
in pain . . .

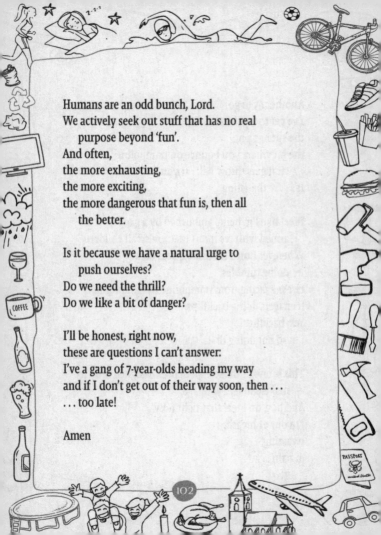

Humans are an odd bunch, Lord.
We actively seek out stuff that has no real
    purpose beyond 'fun'.
And often,
the more exhausting,
the more exciting,
the more dangerous that fun is, then all
    the better.

Is it because we have a natural urge to
    push ourselves?
Do we need the thrill?
Do we like a bit of danger?

I'll be honest, right now,
these are questions I can't answer:
I've a gang of 7-year-olds heading my way
and if I don't get out of their way soon, then . . .
. . . too late!

Amen

For your own reflections and prayers

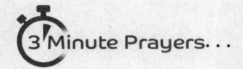

3'Minute Prayers. . .

Before I Sleep
1501601

For the Morning
1501603

For Coffee Breaks
1501605

For Coffee For Grandparents
1501606

For the Evening
1501607

www.kevinmayhew.com